Dwight Eisenhower
Planner, Leader, President

Dwight Eisenhower
Planner, Leader, President

by Sue Hendrix
illustrated by Harold Henriksen

Creative Education
Mankato, Minnesota 56001

Published by Creative Education, 123 South Broad Street,
P. O. Box 227, Mankato, Minnesota 56001
Copyright © 1974 by Creative Education. No part of this book may be reproduced in any form without written permission from the publisher. International copyrights reserved in all countries. Printed in the United States.
Distributed by Childrens Press. 1224 West Van Buren Street, Chicago, Illinois 60607

Library of Congress Numbers: 74-19176   ISBN: 0-87191-409-3
Library of Congress Cataloging in Publication Data
Hendrix, Sue.   Dwight D. Eisenhower.
SUMMARY: A biography of the commanding general of the Allied forces in Europe in World War II who became the thirty-fourth President of the United States.
1. Eisenhower, Dwight David, Pres. U.S., 1890-1969—Juvenile literature.
(1. Eisenhower, Dwight David, Pres. U.S., 1890-1969. 2. Presidents)
I. Henriksen, Harold, illus. II. Title.
E836.H37   973.921'092'4 (B) (92) 74-19176   ISBN 0-87191-409-3

INTRODUCTION

    Dwight D. Eisenhower was a soldier who hated war and a president who disliked politics. During World War II he commanded over 4 million men. Under his direction, the largest invasion army in the history of man freed Europe from Hitler's control. As president, Eisenhower brought a sense of security and peace to the country.
    Eisenhower was born in a small Kansas town at the turn of the century. He often referred to Abilene, Kansas, as "the heart of America." Dwight's childhood is a fascinating story of a mischievous boy growing up in a very religious family. Throughout his life Eisenhower lived by the values he learned in Abilene.

Dwight Eisenhower
Planner, Leader, President

The people of Abilene knew Dwight Eisenhower. He had grown up in the small Kansas town. As a man he had shared the spirit of Abilene with the world. He was dead now, and the whole town deeply felt his absence. Some had waited all night at the old station for the funeral train to arrive. Store owners placed his picture in their windows. Curtains were washed and lawns mowed so everything would look just right for President Eisenhower's last return.

Dwight Eisenhower made Abilene seem all right. He called it the Heart of America. The town was too honest, too straightforward, too neighborly, too simple to fit in with the complicated world of the late 60's. But he had taken the values of Abilene with him all the way to the presidency, and he had told the whole world that the Abilene way is a good way of life.

David Eisenhower had brought his family to Abilene in 1892 when Dwight was only 2. David had grown up in the area; but after the birth of his two oldest sons, Arthur and Edgar, the family moved to Texas where David found work as a mechanic. When David returned to Abilene, he managed to find work at the Belle Springs Creamery.

The family moved into a house near the town's new railroad. The home reflected David and Ida's strong beliefs. They had both grown up in the Church of the River Brethren, a group that lived a strong and simple life in the traditions of the Pennsylvania Dutch.

When David took Ida as his bride, he became supreme head of the family. Dwight later referred to him as "the bread winner, Supreme Court, and Lord High Executioner." David made sure his boys lived by the Bible; and when they didn't, a rod was always waiting. In Abilene the Eisenhowers had three more sons—Milton, Roy, and Earl.

David and Ida believed in self-discipline. They would often say "one should behave properly, not out of fear, but because it is the right thing to do." The 6 boys took the lesson seriously, but they often had different ideas about just what was the right thing. The family may have been very religious, but there was never the silence of a church in the house. The house was always filled with noise.

Ida would rotate the household jobs. Each boy had to take his turn at the worst and the best chores. While none of them liked doing housework no one ever felt discriminated against.

When Dwight was about 8, he had to learn to cook. His mother was quarantined upstairs with Dwight's brother Milton. Milton had scarlet fever, and it was necessary to separate him from the rest of the family. Dwight took over the kitchen. His mother would shout directions to him from her bedroom, and he would try to carry them out in the kitchen. By the time Milton was well, Dwight had become a good cook.

All the Eisenhower boys were encouraged to stand on their own two feet. If they earned money at odd jobs around town, they were allowed to spend it as they wished.

One day Dwight and Edgar, who were good friends as well as brothers, got a job digging a cistern. Edgar, being older, took the easier job of loosening the earth with a pick. Dwight got the job of shoveling out the dirt. After putting up with the situation for most of the day, Dwight talked his brother into letting him have a turn with the pick. Dwight raised the pick high in the air, and with all his strength missed the hole and accidently ran the pick through the side of Edgar's foot. Edgar shouted, "Dwight, clean through my new 24-cent socks."

Ida hated violence and tried to instill that value in the boys. She was not always successful. The boys would never pass up a good fight. Ida's convictions were so strong that later she would actively protest against World War I.

Ike, as his friends now called him, was an excellent poker player by the time he reached high school. He mastered the art of playing percentages. He rarely lost.

David and Ida encouraged their boys to get a good education. They felt that anyone who really wanted an education could get it. Ike and Edgar worked out a plan whereby Ike would work for 2 years and help put Edgar through college; then Edgar would help Ike. Edgar wanted to go into a business. Ike hoped to someday be an engineer.

After high school Ike took whatever jobs he could find. He shoveled coal, harvested the crops, and worked as a night foreman at the creamery. When Ike started work at the creamery, he was paid 10 cents an hour. His main job was to haul 300-pound blocks of ice. The creamery account books show that he was once docked 20 cents for eating ice cream on the job.

Two years after high school a friend told Ike about the possibilities of getting a free education at the U.S. service academies. Ike spent the whole summer studying for the exams.

He took the exams for both Annapolis and West Point. He scored first in his district for Annapolis and second for West Point. Ike lost the Annapolis appointment because he was 21, a year older than the age limit. The boy who had placed first for West Point was disqualified because he could not meet the physical requirements. Ike was notified that he had received the appointment.

It was difficult for David and Ida to see their son join the Army. While Dwight had been carrying ice at the creamery, they had become very involved in a religious group that strongly opposed war. In the end, they let Dwight go. Ida cried that day.

West Point, New York, was a long way from Abilene. During the first days at the Academy Ike had to keep reminding himself that it was a free education, and perhaps even with all the regulations it was a bargain.

One of the first lessons Ike learned was that all cadets salute all officers. While walking down the street one day Ike met the most decorated person he had ever seen. He snapped to attention and saluted. There was no response. He saluted again. Still no response. Just then the rest of the band appeared, and he realized that he had been saluting a drum major.

All the regulations of a military academy were very foreign to a country boy. Going from cover-alls to fancy uniforms was a big step. He could never keep his hat on straight or his shoes shined. He was forever getting demerits for neglecting some rule or other.

If it had not been for his infectious smile and winning personality, Ike probably never would have made it through West Point. In his first years at the academy he always seemed to be in trouble with upper classmen.

One day Ike and a friend were found guilty of breaking a rule. A corporal ordered them to report to his room in "full dress coats." At the appointed time they put on the coats, which were cut straight across the waist with long tails in the back. They wore nothing else. The upperclassman was furious and ordered them to return in full uniform. They returned and spent the rest of the hot summer evening standing at attention.

Ike loved sports and had hoped to play football for West Point. He weighed only 152 pounds and was unable to convince the coach that he was what the team needed. During the year he worked out and was able to gain 20 pounds.

The second year he made first string and played in all the games. While working out for the final game of the season against Navy, Ike twisted his knee. He was hospitalized for a few days.

After being released from the hospital, Ike was doing some required exercises on a horse. One of the exercises was to jump from the horse just as it was leaping a small hurdle. When Ike tried the exercise, his injured knee collapsed and twisted behind him.

Back in the hospital, it took 4 days for the doctor to

straighten out Ike's knee. From that time on Ike was not permitted to play sports. He continued to support the academy's teams by helping as coach, umpire, and at times cheerleader.

Ike's favorite pastime was poker. He rarely went to the academy dances. When there was a dance where food was served, Ike and his friends might break away from their game long enough to raid the food table.

One night when Ike was on the way to the food table, a young lady asked him to dance. His understanding of dance was very different from that of the more restrained easterners. He grabbed the girl and with giant steps whirled her around the room. After the dance he was warned by one of the officers not to dance in such a scandalous way again.

A few months later, Ike met the girl again; and forgetting the warning, he once again swung her around the room. This time he was called before the Commandant. He was demoted from sergeant to private and ordered to his barracks for a month. Then once again his knee began to cause him trouble, and Ike spent his month of punishment in the hospital.

Many men had been released from the Academy for less serious injuries than Ike's. But his personality and ability to lead men managed to keep him there.

Just before graduation Ike was called before Colonel Shaw, the head of the school's medical department. "Cadet

Eisenhower, it is questionable whether we can grant you a commission because of your knee," Shaw said. "You would get your diploma, of course, but we mustn't put a burden on the government with a serious medical problem."

"That's okay," Ike replied, "I always thought I might like to go to the Argentine."

This was the first time the doctor had met someone who was not upset by this kind of news. He called Ike back again a few days later. "Perhaps if you would apply for the Coast Artillery, we could recommend a commission."

"No," Ike replied.

Once more Ike was called to Colonel Shaw's office. "I've been reviewing your record and find your football injury was aggravated by a riding accident. Now if you'll not request mounted service, I will recommend a commission."

Ike was pleased with the Colonel's decision and quickly agreed to the conditions. When it came time to fill out the choices on his duty request form, Ike listed Infantry, Infantry, Infantry.

At graduation, Ike was in the top two-thirds of his class in studies and close to the bottom in conduct. He graduated with the same rank that he had had when he entered.

The class of 1915 was unique in the history of West Point. Out of the 164 graduates, 59 men eventually became generals. Two of them, Eisenhower and Omar Bradley, made the rank of 5-star general. Only 9 men have made this rank in the history of the United States.

Ike went home to Abilene for the first real vacation he had had in 4 years. It was a good feeling to be back with his people. Many of his friends were married or had left town for bigger cities. But the spirit of simple, honest friendship was still there.

Ike anxiously awaited word of his first assignment. He had hoped that he would be stationed in the Philippines, but the Army chose to send him to Fort Sam Houston, at San Antonio, Texas.

At Fort Sam, Ike met Mamie Doud. She was at the base with her parents, visiting friends. Ike and Mamie soon became friends. Sometimes she would follow him as he made his rounds of the base. By winter they were engaged; and on July 1, 1916, they were married.

A year after their marriage, the United States entered World War I. Eisenhower's ability to organize and lead men was beginning to be recognized. He was given a series of assignments to help train the troops for war.

Each time Ike requested active duty in Europe he was given a new assignment in the States. He felt that if his miltary career was to continue to advance, he needed the experience of the battlefield.

At the end of the war Eisenhower was given the Distinguished Service Medal for his work in training 600 officers and 9,000 men at Camp Colt, in Pennsylvania.

After helping discharge troops, Ike was assigned to Camp Meade in Maryland. It was some time before he could find living quarters for Mamie and their small son Icky. Ike temporarily moved into the bachelor quarters and spent his free time winning at poker. He still played strictly by percentages and almost always won. Eventually, he stopped playing with anyone in the Army. He found that too many of his men were losing more than they could afford.

During this time at Camp Meade Eisenhower met George Patton. Ike and Patton began exploring better ways to use the tank as a weapon. During World War I the tank was a small, slow-moving vehicle. It was a good shield for foot soldiers but had little attack power. Ike and Patton tried to develop a vehicle that would be fast moving and have a great deal of attack power.

Mamie and Icky were finally able to join Dwight on base. It was a happy time. Little Icky loved the activity of the base, and the men would often take him along on drills.

A girl from town was hired to help Mamie. Although the girl seemed healthy, she had just recovered from scarlet fever and was still a carrier of the disease. Icky caught the disease and soon died. The loss of their son was a tragedy that the Eisenhowers were never able to forget. Four years later their second son, John, was born.

After Icky's death, Ike worked harder than ever; but his efforts often went unnoticed. His advancement was very slow.

In 1922, Ike was assigned to Panama under the command of General Fox Connors. Connors soon became a major influence in Ike's life. He introduced Ike to a whole new dimension of war. Connors taught Ike how to plan battles. Soon Ike became fascinated with military strategy. He spent a great deal of time studying the great battles of history.

With Connors' help, Eisenhower was admitted to the Command and General Staff School. No longer a disinterested student, Ike graduated first in his class. He also attended the War College in Washington, D.C.

After developing a guide book of World War I battlefields in France, Eisenhower returned to Washington. He was assigned to the staff of General MacArthur. Two years later, in 1935, Ike went with MacArthur to the Philippines. Their task was to organize the Philippine army and to develop a plan for the defense of the islands.

While in the Philippines, Ike learned to fly a plane. He enjoyed flying; but since he was 46, his reflexes were not so fast as those of the younger men who were taking lessons.

When Ike returned to the United States in 1938, he felt that it was only a matter of time until the United States would be drawn into war with Germany. His belief was not always shared by other officers. Many began calling him, "Alarmist Ike."

In 1941, Lieutenant Colonel Eisenhower was appointed Third Army Chief of Staff. One of his first tasks was to organize maneuvers for 270,000 troops in Louisiana. Army Chief of Staff George Marshall attended the maneuvers and was very much impressed with Eisenhower's ability. Eisenhower was still not generally well known. One of the photos taken during the maneuvers lists him as, "Lieutenant Colonel Ersenbeing."

Five days after the Japanese bombed the Navy fleet at Pearl Harbor, Marshall called Eisenhower to Washington. Marshall asked Ike to develop a plan for organizing the American troops in Europe. Three days after handing the plan to Marshall, Ike was appointed Commanding General of the European Forces.

When he went home that evening, he told Mamie that he would be leaving for London next week to assume command.

"Command of what?" Mamie asked.

Ike answered, "Of the whole shebang."

When Eisenhower took command, Europe was under the control of the Germans, Rommel's army controlled the

deserts of North Africa, and the Japanese were in control of the Pacific.

Eisenhower's first objective was to take control of North Africa. His staff in London began planning the attack. They worked 7 days a week, 18 hours a day. Ike constantly emphasized the importance of cooperation between the American and the British armies.

Ike understood the importance of the English and the American armies working together. His staff was made up of officers from both countries. All decisions were made only after both sides fully understood the problem. When necessary, Ike had access to both President Roosevelt and England's Prime Minister Winston Churchill.

Africa was successfully taken, and it provided a base

to move across the Mediterranean Sea to Italy. Whenever Eisenhower moved from command post to command post, he always took his Scottish terrier, Telek, with him. He said that the dog was someone he could talk to and not mention the war.

During the invasion of Italy Ike met with Roosevelt and Churchill. The purpose of the meeting was to plan for the invasion of Europe across the English Channel. The plan was called "Operation Overlord." Originally Roosevelt had planned to put General Marshall in charge of the operation, but he later decided that, "it might be dangerous to monkey with a winning team." He gave the command to Ike.

Ike returned to England to prepare for the largest invasion in the history of man. His greatest task was to organize the armies of many different nations into a single fighting force.

It was a difficult task. His personality helped reduce the problems which arose between armies. Churchill called Eisenhower a "creative, constructive, and combining genius." For months Ike practically lived in his office. He was in constant phone contact with world leaders and the field armies.

The success of "Operation Overlord" depended on calm seas and a clear, moonless night. Meteorologists recommended the first week in June, 1944. An invasion army of 11,000 airplanes, 5,000 ships, and more than 1,000,000 men gathered on the coast of England.

As the target date for June 5th drew near, Ike moved his command post to an English coastal town which was to be a major loading port for the army. Ike spent as much time as possible talking with the men who had assembled for the invasion.

On June 3rd the skies darkened, and a great storm arose. The invasion was delayed. The next day the weather reports predicted a 36-hour lull in the storm. The decision was Ike's. If he ordered the army into battle and the storm came up, thousands of men would be killed for lack of air support. If he did not give the order, the same weather conditions might not exist for possibly a year. The room was silent. Then Ike raised his head and said, "We'll go."

That night, Ike went to the airfield where the paratroopers anxiously awaited the signal to depart. Both Ike and the men knew that casualties might run as high as 70 per cent. Ike moved among the men, talking about everything from poker to the fear of dying. One of the men said to Ike, "Now quit worrying, General. We'll take care of this thing for you." Ike stayed with the men until the last plane took off.

The first wave of troops crossed the channel at 6:30 A.M., June 6, 1944. Eisenhower studied the dispatches all day. On some of the beaches the landing went smoothly. On others the fighting was bloody, and at times it was questionable whether the army could hold them. On Omaha Beach over 2,500 men died before the beach was taken.

Ike had prepared two announcements — one if the army was successful, another if the army failed. In his announcement of success he gave full credit to the courage of the men; in the announcement he never had to use, he had accepted full responsibility for the failure.

At first, the army's advance across France was slow, but by late summer Ike was able to move his headquarters across the channel to Normandy.

While in Normandy a group of grateful farmers brought Ike a cow so that he could have fresh milk. For a long time the general's aides deliberated over the problem of milking a cow. Finally, Ike appeared, found a pail and proceeded to give his staff a lesson in how to milk a cow.

The advance across Europe was going well. Ike was able to spend a good deal of time with his troops. Four million men were under his command, and he was able to let them know that each man was important to him.

Eleven months after the first landing on the beaches, the German army surrendered. Four months later the Japanese army unconditionally surrendered. The war was over.

After a triumphal return to the United States, Ike returned to Abilene. His mother was 83. His brothers returned to share in the reunion. A reporter asked Ida what she thought of her son. With a famous Eisenhower smile she answered, "Which one?"

In 1948, after helping discharge the army, Ike retired from active duty. He accepted the position of president of

Columbia University in New York. He remained president of the university for only 2 years. In 1950 he became commander of the European defense army known as NATO (North Atlantic Treaty Organization).

Since 1943 both political parties had been trying to get Eisenhower to run for President. He had repeatedly refused to consider the idea. Ike believed that military men should stay out of politics.

In 1951, Robert Taft was a leading contender for the Republican presidential nomination. Taft strongly opposed the support the United States was giving to Europe. Ike strongly opposed Taft's position and agreed to run for the presidency on the Republican ticket. He returned to Abilene to announce his candidacy.

Millions of Americans believed that Ike's Abilene character was what the country needed. He was a simple, yet firm man, with a genuine faith in people. He was determined to be above politics and political parties. People voted for Ike and not for a political leader. He was elected by a larger vote than any president before him. Ike was 62 when he took office.

Eisenhower was a greater person than he was a president. He ran the White House as he had run the Army. He relied heavily on his staff; and when things went wrong, the public would blame his staff — never Ike.

During his first term as president, he ended the Korean War and brought this country a feeling of security that it had not had in many years. He often dealt with problems by ignoring them.

Twice during his first term, Ike suffered heart attacks. Still, ignoring the advice of his doctors, Ike decided to run for a second term. He said that he felt a need to finish the job he had started.

The people re-elected Ike by a wider margin than before. His second term was filled with more problems than his first. His health was one of them. A year after the election, Ike suffered a stroke, and his speech was affected.

The Russians were a major threat to America's feeling of security. They were becoming more aggressive in Europe and challenged America's scientific leadership by launching the world's first space capsule.

Racial injustice was becoming a major problem. After years of neglect the courts and Congress took the first steps toward ending segregation. Ike, believing that integration could not be accomplished by passing laws, did not actively try to root out racial injustice. He did however support the decision of Congress and the courts. When the Little Rock school system refused to admit blacks into their schools, Eisenhower sent government troops into the city to enforce a court order.

The country was suffering from serious economic problems. Since the great depression of the '30s the country had not known such a crisis. Workers lost their jobs, and it was difficult for families to pay their bills.

Toward the end of his second term Ike toured the capitals of the world and was cheered by millions of people. Americans and the world still loved the man.

In his last official speech to the American people Ike warned of the dangers of allowing the military to become too strong. He saw the problems that would arise if a country's industry and military power worked too closely together.

When Ike left office he was 70, the oldest president in the history of the United States. His successor, John F. Kennedy, admired the lively spirit which Ike still radiated.

Ike moved with Mamie to the only home they had ever owned. It was an old 80-acre farm in Gettysburg, Pennsylvania. Ike said, "I wanted to take a piece of ground like this that had been sort of worn out through improper use and try to restore it. When I die, I'm going to leave a piece of ground better than I found it."

Ike now had time to relax. He was able to spend more time fishing and golfing than when he was president. Ike and Mamie enjoyed having their grandchildren come to the farm.

At times of national crises, both presidents Kennedy and Johnson called on Ike for advice. His years of experience and common sense helped clarify the problems facing the nation.

Frequently Ike and Mamie would return to Abilene. They would window shop, talk with old friends, and examine the progress on the Eisenhower Center.

The Eisenhower Center was built next to Ike's childhood home. The center has a museum, a library, and small chapel. Over 16.5 million pages of documents are housed in the center. When the chapel was finished, Ike and Mamie had the body of their son Icky moved to the chapel.

Ike's retirement years were full and active. His writing, library work, and visits from friends and leaders filled his days. However, his health was failing. He was frequently admitted to Walter Reed Army Hospital for heart problems.

Early in 1969 Ike entered the hospital for the last time. He was 79. Each day the medical bulletins issued from the hospital grew more discouraging. Papers around the world carried headlines that the General was dying. On March 28, a representative of the hospital announced that Ike was dead. "General of the Army Dwight David Eisenhower, 34th President of the United States, died quietly at 12:25 this noon, after a long and heroic battle against overwhelming illness. His passing was peaceful, and he experienced no distress."

Ike's last words were, "I've always loved my wife. I've always loved my children. I've always loved my grandchildren. And I have always loved my country."

The flags of the nation were lowered to half mast. From around the world leaders began to assemble to salute the great general of World War II for the last time. Nearly 200 kings, presidents, premiers, and high military officials from

78 nations came to the state funeral.

The body of Ike was put in an $85 coffin and placed in the rotunda of the capital where more than 55,000 people silently passed by. A eulogy was delivered by President Nixon.

"He had the great leader's capacity to bring out the best in people," President Nixon said. "Almost nobody ever hated him because he himself was a man who did not know how to hate. He exemplified what millions of parents hoped that their sons would be — strong, courageous, honest, and compassionate."

After the state funeral the body went by train back home to Abilene. Mamie rode in the same Santa Fe car that she and Ike had used when they returned home to announce his candidacy for president.

Eisenhower had requested that his funeral be simple. However, the military had been planning for it for 2 years. The plan was called "Operation Kansas." Every detail had been noted in a 100-page outline. There was even a scale model of Abilene so that the procession's route might be carefully studied. In its own strange way the Army with its planning was honoring a great general.

It was a sunny day when Ike returned to Abilene for the last time. Old friends gathered with family and dignitaries to hear words and to pray. The body of the general was placed next to his son in the small chapel just across the way from the house where Ike had grown up.

Sue Hendrix

Sue Hendrix is a person of indeterminate age, or so she hopes. She lives in Minneapolis, Minnesota, with two really special children — Volney, 13, and Abbie, 12. Sue has been in some form of education most of her life. At present her chief excitement is the formation of and the work in a new Open School. There she pursues her ideas and interests in crafts, animals, plants, and the growth of "OKness" in people.

While Sue and the kids are schooling it, Toulouse and Amiess, the brown poodles, take charge of the house. The snake and fishes are on their own.

Harold Henriksen

Harold was born in St. Paul, Minnesota and has lived there most of his life. He attended the School of the Associated Arts in St. Paul.

Even while serving in the Army, Harold continued to keep alive his desire to become an artist. In 1965 he was a winner in the All Army Art Contest.

After the Army, Harold returned to Minnesota where he worked for several art studios in the Minneapolis-St. Paul area. In 1967 he became an illustrator for one of the largest art studios in Minneapolis.

During 1971 Harold and his wife traveled to South America where he did on-the-spot drawings for a year. Harold, his wife and daughter Maria now live in Minneapolis where he works as a free lance illustrator.

close ups

Walt Disney
Bob Hope
Duke Ellington
Dwight Eisenhower
Coretta King
Pablo Picasso
Ralph Nader
Bill Cosby
Dag Hammarskjold
Sir Frederick Banting
Mark Twain
Beatrix Potter

92
EIS   Hendrix, Sue
AUTHOR
       Dwight Eisenhower
TITLE

DATE DUE	BORROWER'S NAME	ROOM NUMBER

92
EIS
Hendrix, Sue
    Dwight Eisenhower